GANDHI
The Mahatma

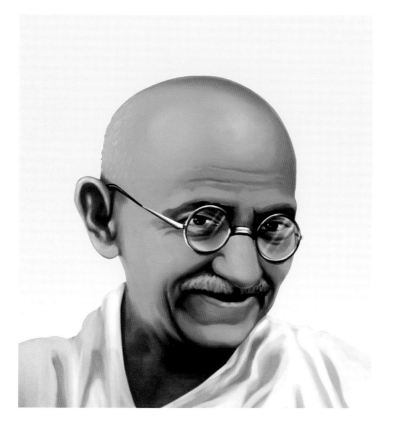

An imprint of Om Books International

Reprinted in 2016

An imprint of Om Books International

Corporate & Editorial Office
A 12, Sector 64, Noida 201 301
Uttar Pradesh, India
Phone: +91 120 477 4100
Email: editorial@ombooks.com
Website: www.ombooksinternational.com

Sales Office
107, Ansari Road, Darya Ganj
New Delhi 110 002, India
Phone: +91 11 4000 9000
Fax: +91 11 2327 8091
Email: sales@ombooks.com
Website: www.ombooks.com

ISBN : 978-93-80070-48-3

Printed in India

10 9 8 7 6 5 4 3

Contents

FATHER OF THE NATION

Mohandas Karamchand Gandhi, popularly known as Mahatma Gandhi, is often referred to as the 'Father of the Nation' of India. Mahatma Gandhi believed in the concept of ahimsa or non-violence. And it was the path of ahimsa that he walked in his endeavours to free the nation from British rule. Gandhiji always spoke the truth and lived a very simple life. His philosophy of non-violence and his Satyagraha (a non-violent protest that demands truth) has inspired political activists throughout the world.

5

GANDHIJI'S BIRTH

Mohandas Karamchand Gandhi was born on October 2, 1869, in a Vaishya family in Porbander, a town in Kathiawar district, in the state of Gujarat. His father's name was Karamchand Gandhi and his mother's name was Putlibai. For several generations, Gandhiji's ancestors had served as Chief Ministers in the Kathiawar States located on the western coast of India. His father, too, was the Chief Minister of Porbander and a member of the Rajasthan court. Sadly, when Gandhiji was just sixteen years old, his father died. Then, four years later, he lost his mother, too.

CHILDHOOD DAYS

Gandhiji loved and respected his parents a lot. Thus, on their insistence, he agreed to be married in May 1883. He was only a little more than thirteen years old then! His wife, Kasturba, was as old as him, and the two became good friends quite soon.

Gandhiji's family was strictly vegetarian. When he was young, Gandhiji once ate meat out of curiosity and was very sorry later.

And so, when he was leaving for London to pursue his higher studies, Gandhiji promised his mother that he would abstain from eating meat and drinking alcohol. He kept his promise and remained a vegetarian all his life.

Later, he even wrote a book, titled *The Moral Basis of Vegetarianism* on the subject.

Gandhiji completed his primary education in India. In September 1888, he went to London to study law. In 1893, he moved to South Africa to practise law.

RACISM IN SOUTH AFRICA

When Gandhiji was in South Africa, he faced a lot of racial discrimination. In those days, South Africa was also under British rule. The use of public property was divided according to the people of different races.

Once, Gandhiji was travelling by train. Unaware of the separate compartments meant for the British, Indians and Africans on the train, he boarded a compartment meant only for the British.

A British man saw Gandhiji and angrily pushed him out of the moving train! This incident disturbed Gandhiji immensely. Later, he was even stopped from entering many hotels because of his race. These events fostered a feeling of nationalism in Gandhiji and he decided to fight against racial discrimination.

In 1894, Gandhiji founded the National Indian Congress to fight discrimination faced by Indian traders in South Africa. Based on his policy of non-violence and his determination, Gandhiji became the first non-white lawyer to be admitted to the bar in South Africa!

FAMILY LIFE

Mahatma Gandhi and Kasturba were blessed with four sons, namely, Harilal, Manilal, Ramdas and Devdas. Kasturba often joinedGandhiji in his political protests.

In 1897, she even travelled to South Africa to be with her husband. Then, in 1913, while protesting against the inhuman working conditions of Indians in South Africa, Kasturba was arrested. As a result, she was sentenced to three months in a prison where the inmates were subjected to difficult labour.

Later, when they returned to India, she would often participate in protests in place of her husband while he was under arrest. In 1915, when Gandhiji returned to India to support the indigo planters, Kasturba accompanied him to the villages. She taught hygiene, discipline, reading and writing to the women and children there.

The constant strain because of the arrests made during Quit India Movement's arrests and the hard life at Sabarmati Ashram had an adverse effect on Kasturba's health. She suffered from chronic bronchitis and fell sick during one of her imprisonments. Her sickness was further complicated by a serious bout of pneumonia. Later, in January 1944, she suffered two heart attacks. She never could recover completely, and on February 22, 1944, she died in Gandhiji's arms in prison, in Pune.

NON-VIOLENT PROTEST

When the country faced extreme oppression from the British rule, Gandhiji used an entirely new way of revolt. He based his struggle for freedom on the principles of truth and non-violence. This was called *Satyagraha* (a non-violent protest demanding truth). A person who practises *Satyagraha* was known as a *Satyagrahi*. According to *Satyagraha*, one must not use physical force or violence to fight injustice.

According to Gandhian philosophy, a *Satyagrahi* does not hurt or destroy his oppressor in any way. Without being aggressive, a *Satyagrahi* can win any battle, just through non-violence.

A *Satyagrahi* appeals to the conscience of the oppressor. He never uses force or violence to make others accept the truth. He persuades everyone, including the oppressor, to see the truth through dialogue.

24

TOLSTOY FARM

When he was in South Africa, Gandhiji brought all the people of his community to live together. He wanted them to live just like brothers in a foreign land. For this, he created a community living arrangement at a farm in South Africa and called it 'Tolstoy Farm'.

Tolstoy Farm was named after the Russian writer Leo Tolstoy. Gandhiji and Tolstoy corresponded through letters and shared ideas. Soon, they grew to respect and admire each other immensely.

BACK TO INDIA

Gandhiji lived in South Africa for 20 years. During this period, he developed a strong system of nonviolent protest. For his services of recruiting Indian volunteers for the Ambulance Corps during the Boer War in 1906, he was awarded the War Medal.

When Gandhiji returned to India in January 1915, he realised the need for eradicating racial discrimination. Moreover, the desire to gain independence from foreign rule inspired him to become involved in politics. However, even then, he did not participate directly in politics.

Gandhiji started visiting Indian villages to understand the problems of the people. Wherever he went, he tried to educate people to help them overcome their problems.

Through all his travels, Gandhiji was very sad to see the plight of Indians in villages and small towns and the extreme poverty they lived in.

CHAMPARAN AND KHEDA

Once, in 1914, Gandhiji was delivering a speech in a village in the Champaran district of Bihar. Just then, a farmer stood up from the audience and accused Gandhiji of never actually understanding the problems faced by the people in their daily life.

He also told Gandhiji about the harsh treatment the British meted out to the farmers. They were being forced to grow crops like indigo and opium on their land. Once such crops were grown in a field, no other crop could be grown on the same land for several years until natural processes replenished the soil.

This meant that those who would grow these crops would not have any means of living in the future, because their land would become worthless. Gandhiji was shocked to hear this! He, at once, inspired the villagers to stand up and fight for their rights.

However, since he was against violence, he urged people to use methods of non-violence, that is, Satyagraha. Hence, this movement was a Satyagraha against the oppressive indigo plantation.

Moving from one Indian State to another, Gandhiji reached his home State, Gujarat. Here, the peasants of the Kheda District approached Gandhiji with their problem. The farmers were distressed because the British Government had imposed heavy taxes on them. Sadly, a drought had struck the nation that year. The crops had failed and the farmers found it difficult to pay taxes, since they did not have enough money even to survive! Gandhiji forced them to launch a no tax campaign to make the government realise that the farmers were poor. Thus, the revenue collection norms could be relaxed in the district. Gandhiji kept moving within the country.

PROBLEMS OF MILL WORKERS

In 1918, Gandhiji reached Ahmedabad, now the capital of Gujarat. At that time, Ahmedabad was a hub of textile mills.

Since it was located near the coastline, many foreign investors had set up their industries and mills in Ahmedabad. The workers employed in these factories were not given proper wages and holidays.

They were not allowed to visit their families residing in nearby villages. The mill workers were troubled and angry. Gandhiji organised a *Satyagraha* movement and inspired them all to fight for their rights.

Gandhiji's constant efforts to help the common man earned him the respect and love of Indians. The people lovingly addressed him as *Mahatma* (great soul) and *Bapu* (father).

STRUGGLE FOR INDEPENDENCE

Through his travels, the keenly observant Gandhiji realised that all Indians wanted freedom. Thus, he joined the struggle for independence. He decided to start a nationwide movement.

First, he brought together all the communities of India under the common umbrella of a united

struggle for independence.He wanted the people of India to forget their religious differences and fight together. According to him, the country belonged to every Indian and each individual was to fight for its freedom.

Gandhiji said that for every Indian, the independence of India needed to be of primary importance. Then, the welfare of the State in which one lived. An individual's religion was to be of least significance. Thus, people needed to first fight for their country, then their State and only then for

their religion. He emphasised this in his book *Hind Swaraj*. He said that the esteemed spiritual leaders like Jesus Christ and Prophet Mohammad used religion to bring peace to the world.

Gandhiji was a practitioner of *ahimsa* and swore to speak the truth at all times. He also advocated that others do the same. He lived in a humble, self-sufficient residential community. He wore a traditional Indian *dhoti* and shawl, woven with the yarn he had handspun on a *charkha* (spinning wheel). He ate simple vegetarian food. Eventually, he adopted a diet of just fruits. However, sometimes, he also undertook long fasts as a means of both self-purification and social protest.

CHARKHA AND KHADI

Gandhiji advocated the boycott of machine-made clothes. He believed that since machines came into use in India, a very large number of labourers became unemployed.

He started spinning *khadi* on his *charkha* and making clothes with the woven fabric. This was inexpensive and suitable for poor Indians. Gandhiji worked on his charkha and encouraged all Indians to do the same by setting an example.

Spinning *khadi* on a *charkha* became very popular. Many Indians started spinning the *charkha* and producing their own cloth. The charkha became the symbol of self-reliance and impacted the British immensely.

NON-COOPERATION MOVEMENT

Gandhiji conceptualised the Non-Cooperation Movement in 1920 to resist the dominance of the British Government. The Non-Cooperation Movement was a non-violent movement that was followed all over India. Gandhiji strictly advised all the Indians,

who participated in the Movement, to observe truth and non-violence.

He decided that people should give up the titles given to them by the British. They would also boycott civil services like the army, as well as all British-run schools, and also foreign goods. He urged people to boycott the British courts and establish their own private judicial courts.

People were instructed to use Swadeshi (goods manufactured in one's own country) clothes and boycott the foreign clothes and other items. In the first month of the Movement, approximately nine thousand students left schools and colleges and joined national institutions. During this period, about eight hundred national institutions were set up all over the country. This educational boycott was quite successful, particularly in the state of West Bengal.

The boycott of foreign clothing, was the most successful outcome of Non-Cooperation Movement. Gandhiji promoted khadi to boycott imported clothes. Soon, khadi became a symbol of nationalism.

The Movement continued from September 1920 to February 1922. In 1922, at Chauri Chaura, a peaceful demonstration in a market suddenly became violent. Mahatma Gandhi was in support of complete non-violence. The Chauri Chaura incident upset him and he decided to call off the Movement.

Thus, on February 12, 1922, the Non-Cooperation Movement came to an end. Gandhiji was arrested and imprisoned for two years. Though the Movement failed, Indians awakened to fight for their freedom and to stand against the British. The Movement taught the Indians fearlessness.

THE FIRST ROUND TABLE CONFERENCE

After the conclusion of the Non-Cooperation Movement, the British asked the Congressmen to attend a Round Table Conference. Gandhiji knew that the British wanted to divide the Congress. Thus, he was against it, and threatened to fast until death if any Congressman attended the conference.

The First Round Table Conference was held in London on November 12, 1930. From India, some princes, their advisors, a couple of millionaires and many rich landlords participated in the Conference.

However, all Congressmen boycotted the First Round Table Conference. The Conference was a failure.

GANDHI-IRWIN PACT

Gandhiji wanted to liberate all the communities in India. So, he wrote a letter to Viceroy Irwin, wherein, he put forth 11 demands. These demands included abolition of salt tax, abandoning emigration act and tax relaxation.

He included the demands of as many communities as possible. He wanted to make the letter versatile and wanted it to voice the needs of all possible communities of India.

In his letter, Gandhiji also said that if the demands laid down were not met by March 11, 1930, the Congress party would start a Civil Disobedience Movement. Through this Movement, Indians would boycott every item manufactured by the British. They would also disobey the colonial civil laws.

These demands were not met by 11th March. Gandhiji decided to start the Movement as planned. Since, the abolition of the tax levied on salt was a very important agenda of his letter to Irwin, Gandhiji decided to focus on that first.

DANDI MARCH

Salt is an important commodity for Indians and is used in every dish. The British used this knowledge to earn money by selling salt to Indians.

Therefore, they passed a law, ordering Indians not to produce or sell salt. Everybody had to buy salt from the British. Thus, the British earned a lot of money. Gandhiji decided to disobey this 'salt law'.

He organised a meeting of all the Congress leaders in Sabarmati Ashram. There, they decided to produce salt by boiling sea water. They also wanted to influence other Indians to produce salt.

On March 12, 1930, Gandhiji and his 74 followers started their journey towards the port town of Dandi in Gujarat. The total journey covered 240 miles from their starting point in Sabarmati. They completed ten miles a day and marched for 24 days.

During the march, they stopped and addressed gatherings of followers to garner support for their march. Gandhiji reached Dandi on April 6, 1930.

There, he boiled sea water and obtained salt from it. This was a great triumph for Indians. They enthusiastically cheered for Gandhiji.

This incident also marked a major defeat for the British. They were shocked and angry and started beating the Indians who were rejoicing in front of the salt factories. Many Indians were killed and injured and around one lakh Indians were arrested.

Gandhiji was also arrested. This enraged people across the country and they attacked all British structures. In Sholapur, the workers attacked police posts, municipal buildings and railway stations.

Gandhiji was very troubled by this violence. Thus, he decided to call off the Movement. He signed a pact with Irwin on March 5, 1931. According to this pact, Gandhiji agreed to participate in the Second Round Table Conference. In return, the British agreed to release all the political prisoners.

HARIJANS AND THE POONA PACT

In 1932, Dr. B.R. Ambedkar raised his voice for the people of low castes or *Dalit*s with the support of Mahatma Gandhi. He declared that independence could not be achieved if untouchability was not eliminated from our society. Gandhiji addressed the *Dalit*s with a new name, *Harijan*s, which means the children of God.

He organised a *Satyagraha* Movement so that the people of low castes could be allowed to enter temples and schools. In an attempt to persuade the orthodox Hindus to wipe out the blight of untouchability, Gandhiji undertook a three week fast in the summer of 1933.

Around the same time, the *Dalit*s made a demand for reservation or special privileges. However, Gandhiji was against reservation. Thus, he entered into a pact with Dr. B.R. Ambedkar. This was called the Poona Pact. According to this Pact, reservations were provided to the Dalits in legislative assemblies.

QUIT INDIA MOVEMENT

Gandhi launched the Quit India Movement or the *Bharat Chhodo Andolan* in August 1942. He issued a call for the British to 'Quit India' immediately. He launched the Movement with the aim to make the British leave India.

The slogan of 'Do or Die' was adopted for this purpose. Gandhiji addressed the people, 'We shall do or die. We shall either free India or die in the attempt.'

The British Government was against this Movement and reacted brutally by arresting all Congress leaders, including Gandhiji and his wife Kasturba. As the protests grew, the Government arrested and jailed hundreds of thousands of Indians. Gandhiji was held for two years. Gandhiji's secretary Mahadev Desai died while still in prison. Kasturba also passed away after eighteen months in prison. Towards the end of 1943, the Quit India Movement came to an end.

Gandhiji was released in May 1944 because of failing health. However, he kept up the resistance even after his release. He demanded the complete release of the Congress leaders who were still in prison. Around ten thousand political prisoners were released and the British indirectly confirmed that complete power would soon be transferred to the people of India.

After the Quit India Movement, the intensity of the freedom struggle increased. The entire country

INDIAN INDEPENDENCE

was united in the Movement for freedom. Everyone contributed what they could in the freedom struggle.

The cry of *Poorna Swaraj* or complete independence was raised. After many sacrifices and tireless efforts, India finally became independent on August 15, 1947. Gandhiji's peaceful protests and his non-violent movements helped India attain independence.

Gandhiji was a good writer and authored several books. He edited many newspapers including *Harijan*

GANDHIJI'S WRITINGS

in Gujarati, Hindi and English; *the Indian Opinion* while in South Africa; *Young India* in English; and *Navajivan*, a Gujarati monthly. In addition, he wrote letters to individuals and several newspapers almost every day. He also wrote articles on varied topics, such as vegetarianism, diet, health, religion, rural reforms and on the *Bhagvad Gita*.

Gandhiji wrote several books including an autobiography, *The Story of My Experiments with*

Truth, Satyagraha in South Africa, and a paraphrased Gujarati version of John Ruskin's *Unto This Last*. A bulk of Gandhiji's literary works were written in Gujrati, his mother tongue. He was quite fond of the language. These works were then translated into several other languages.

On the evening of January 30, 1948, Gandhiji was killed by Nathu Ram Godse. He fired three bullets

GANDHIJI'S DEATH

at Gandhiji when Gandhiji was going for a prayer meeting. Gandhiji's efforts to achieve reconciliation between the Hindus and the Muslims eventually led to his death, since Nathu Ram Godse felt that Gandhiji had betrayed the Hindus.

Gandhiji's last words were, 'Hey Ram,' which are inscribed at Raj Ghat in New Delhi, where he was cremated.

That night, Pandit Jawaharlal Nehru addressed the people of India on radio, 'Friends and Comrades, the

light has gone out of our lives and there is darkness everywhere. I do not know what to tell you and how to say it. Our beloved leader, Bapu as we called him, the Father of the Nation, is no more...'

The news of Gandhiji's death left the whole world in mourning. The United Nations lowered their flags

to half-mast. Gandhiji's death was regarded as an international tragedy.

After a few days, Gandhiji's body was cremated in the presence of a large crowd as per

Hindu customs.

Gandhiji remains a great
inspiration not only to India,
but to the entire world. He

is respected as the man who led the Indian independence struggle without resorting to violence; who stood for *ahimsa* with courage, amidst all odds. The thoughts, philosophy and the teachings of Mahatma Gandhi inspire people from all over the world, even after more than six decades of his death.